COMPUTERS

Beeps, Whirs
And Blinking Lights

ABOUT FIRST LOOK BOOKS

A new series designed to teach young readers the fundamentals of computer operation and programming, First Look Books are an ideal resource for parents, teachers and students. Ideas are developed logically, from simple computer concepts to the complexities of the binary number system and programming. Illustrated with dozens of lively drawings, each of the First Look Books helps the young reader progress in learning about computers and how they work.

Each First Look Book may be enjoyed individually or as one in a series.

COMPUTERS
Beeps, Whirs
And Blinking Lights

J. M. Johnston
Illustrated by Len Epstein

Miles Standish Press

BOOKS IN THE "FIRST LOOK" SERIES

Published by
Miles Standish Press, Inc.
37 West Avenue   Wayne, Pennsylvania 19087

Copyright © 1983 by J. M. Johnston

Dell ® TM 681510, Dell Publishing Co., Inc.

ISBN: 0-440-01409-3

First Printing — September 1983

For Arne

What's that you're typing?

It's a report for a class in school on all the things I've learned about computers.

And what have you learned?

Oh, lots. Computers can be used by just about anyone—doctors, policemen, airplane pilots . . . you name it.

They're used in factories to control temperatures and machines, and in schools to teach students, and in banks to figure people's accounts.

And they're used in subways, and post offices, and libraries. . . .

Are you explaining how computers work in your report?

Well, I'm showing how computers are like human brains, because they can add and subtract, and make decisions, and control things. And they use input, *like our eyes and ears, and make* output, *like the things we say and write. And they have* memories *to keep important information.*
But I'm having a little trouble.

What's the problem?

I guess I really don't know what goes on inside a computer—how all those things get done in there.

Well, maybe we should take a little trip inside one and see for ourselves.

I was hoping you would say that! Where do we start?

Right at the heart of the thing—the *CPU*.

You know I'm going to ask what a CPU is.

I'd be disappointed if you didn't. The CPU is where all the real thinking goes on in the computer. It stands for *Central Processing Unit* and it's the part of the computer most like your own brain.

I guess that means every computer has to have one.

That's right. The CPU is the most important part of the computer system, just like your brain is the most important part of your body. You can't do anything without it.

Is the CPU in the same place as the computer's memory?

Not exactly. In your brain, everything is all together in one neat package, but in a computer, things usually come in separate packages.

However, the CPU and memory are very close together, because the CPU uses the information in the computer's memory to do its work.

What kind of work does it do?

The CPU handles those things you were just talking about—arithmetic, control, and making decisions. And the CPU is usually divided into two parts—one part does the arithmetic and decisions, and the other part does the control.

Let's talk about arithmetic first. Most of what this part does is counting and adding. Of course, it also subtracts and multiplies and divides and does lots of other kinds of arithmetic, but counting and adding are the most important.

To understand how the CPU counts and adds, it helps to remember what you and I use when we count and add.

That's easy. We use numbers.

That's right. And a number is made up of symbols. Do you know what a *symbol* is?

In school we learned that a symbol stands for something.

Give me an example.

Well . . . a flag is a symbol because it stands for a country.

Right. When you see the American flag, you think of the United States.

Here are some more symbols. Can you tell me what they stand for?

A church . . . and a barber shop . . . peace . . . and "No Smoking."

Good. And how about this one?

That means wrong, like when you miss a problem on a test.

Can it mean anything else? How about the Roman numeral 10?

And it also means to multiply.

Or it could mean just the letter X in the alphabet.

Lots of X's together means love and kisses.

So some symbols have more than one meaning, don't they? And in a computer, symbols can also have different meanings, depending on how they are used.

Now, numbers are made up of symbols, too. How many different number symbols do we use when we count?

Oh, lots and lots. Thousands!

No. Only ten.

Just ten?

Sure. And here they are:

0 1 2 3 4 5 6 7 8 9

All of the numbers we use are made up of just these ten symbols, by putting them together in different ways:

17   2486   0   999   893702119

Why do you suppose we use ten symbols instead of five, or twenty, or anything else?

Gee, I don't know.

How many fingers do you have?

Ten!

15

And since primitive man probably used his fingers to help him count, like small children do, he probably kept right on using them when he began to write the numbers down. Even Roman numerals come in groups of ten.

Now, the people who built the early computers also tried to use ten symbols. They used gears with ten teeth on them, which had to turn to the right position for each number.

But this was very slow and the gears were always getting stuck. The CPUs in today's computers use *electricity* to count instead of gears. Electricity is extremely fast and it uses only two "fingers."

Huh? What do you mean two fingers?

Well, think of all the very simple electrical appliances around your house, like light bulbs and fans. All you ever do is turn them *on* and *off*, right?

Right.

And to do that, you use a *switch*. Now, inside the CPU are lots of tiny switches—so small that you'd need a microscope to see them.

Each of these switches can be turned on and off very rapidly, millions of times a *second*! And since there are only two positions, the CPU uses the symbol 1 to stand for *on* and the symbol 0 to stand for *off*.

But how can it count and do arithmetic with only a 0 and a 1?

The same way we do with ten symbols. Let's think about that.

We use the symbols 0 through 9 in our counting system, which is called the *decimal* system because "decem" in Latin means "ten." But whenever we count

16

past 9, we run out of symbols, don't we?

So we start putting our symbols together in pairs—two at a time. The number 15, for example, is a 1 and a 5 together. This way, we can write numbers from 10 up through 99. What happens after 99?

We run out of symbols again.

So we start putting three of them together. This gives us the numbers 100 through 999.

Then we put four symbols together, for 1000 through 9999.

Right. Each time we add a symbol, we can make larger and larger numbers. We go from *ones*, to *tens*, to *hundreds*, to *thousands*, and so on.

And that's how we make all the numbers we ever need to use, with only the ten original symbols.

But how does the CPU do it with only two?

The same way. Each time it runs out of symbols, it puts more 0s and 1s together to make bigger numbers.

But it runs out of symbols after "1"!

That's okay. It just uses a pair of symbols to make the number 2, and it's written "10"—which *looks* like "ten," but in a computer it stands for the number 2.

And a 3 is written "11." But now the CPU has already run out of ways to put pairs of symbols together, so it has

to start using three symbols. The number 4, for example, is written "100."

There are several ways to put three symbols together, like "101" for 5 and "110" for 6. But sooner or later, it has to start using four symbols: the number 8 is written "1000." Then five symbols: the number 16 is "10000," and so on.

And that's the way the CPU makes all the numbers it needs for counting, using only the symbols 0 and 1. This is called the *binary* system because "bi" means "two"— like in bicycle, which has two wheels.

But the CPU has to do more than just count, doesn't it? Can it add and subtract with these binary numbers?

Sure—just like we do with decimal numbers. We write:

$$
\begin{array}{r}
8 \\
+\ 6 \\
\hline
14
\end{array}
$$

In binary, we would write:

1000   (which stands for 8)
+ 110   (which stands for 6)
———
1110   (which stands for 14)

Of course, it starts to get a little complicated when you have to subtract or multiply. But the CPU isn't bothered—it just flips those tiny switches, adding and subtracting so fast it would make your head spin.

My head's already spinning just trying to figure out how to read those strings of 0s and 1s.

But you don't have to. The computer always prints its numbers in decimal or some other counting system for people to read.

You mean there are still other counting systems?

Sure. There's *octal*, which uses *eight* symbols— 0 through 7. And there's *hexadecimal*, which uses *sixteen* symbols.

Sixteen? I thought you said there weren't any symbols after 9.

There aren't. So letters from the alphabet are used to stand for 10, 11, 12, 13, 14 and 15. So the hexadecimal symbols are:

0 1 2 3 4 5 6 7 8 9 A B C D E F

For example, the decimal number 2975 would be written "B9F" in hexadecimal.

That looks weird! Does the CPU use octal and hexadecimal?

2975=B9F

No, the CPU uses *only* binary numbers to do all its arithmetic and logic operations.

What's "logic"?

That's the kind of work done by the CPU in making decisions.

But what kind of decisions can the CPU make with only 0 and 1 symbols?

That's easy. Making a decision means asking a question, right? Should I do this or should I do that? And each choice can be answered with a yes or a no. Yes, I should do this . . . or no, I shouldn't do that.

Remember we said that in a computer, symbols often have different meanings? Well, in the logic section the CPU lets the symbol 1 stand for YES, and the symbol 0 stand for NO.

But you can't add a YES and a NO.

The logic section doesn't add—it ANDs.

Huh? How do you AND something?

By using 1 and 0 to mean YES and NO. In the CPU,

	1 (YES)		1 (YES)		0 (NO)		0 (NO)
AND	1 (YES)	AND	0 (NO)	AND	1 (YES)	AND	0 (NO)
	1 (YES)		0 (NO)		0 (NO)		0 (NO)

Notice that you don't always get the same thing when you AND as you do when you add.

I don't get it at all.

Well, let's take an example. Suppose your school gave a prize to anyone who could answer YES to *both* of these questions:

1. Are all your grades A's?
   AND
2. Do you have a perfect attendance record?

If your answers are YES and YES, that's 1 AND 1. If you look back at the chart, you find that 1 AND 1 gives us 1. And since 1 stands for YES, you get a prize.

If *one* of your answers is NO, then that's 1 AND 0 (or 0 AND 1). And that gives us 0, which stands for NO, you *don't* get a prize.

And, of course, if *both* your answers are NO, that's 0 AND 0, which also gives us 0—no prize.

Hey, that's fun! Are there any other logic things we can do with 0s and 1s?

Sure—we can OR them.

How does that work?

Well, 1 is still YES and 0 is still NO. But now,

	1	(YES)		1	(YES)		0	(NO)		0	(NO)
OR	1	(YES)	OR	0	(NO)	OR	1	(YES)	OR	0	(NO)
	1	(YES)		1	(YES)		1	(YES)		0	(NO)

Suppose now that all you needed to earn that prize was to answer YES to *just one* of those same two questions. You could have *either* all A's OR perfect attendance—it isn't necessary to have both.

If you do answer YES and YES, that's 1 OR 1, which gives us 1—YES, you get your prize.

If *one* of your answers is NO, that's 1 OR 0 (or 0 OR 1), which *still* gives us 1 this time, and you *still* get your prize.

If *both* of your answers are NO, then that's 0 OR 0, which gives us 0—no prize.

I like the OR better than the AND—there are more ways to get the prize!

That's true. But the computer isn't interested in prizes. It uses ANDs and ORs to decide things like whether to add or subtract, and what to do with the answers.

How does the CPU know which symbols to add and which ones to AND?

Good question. And the answer is, the control section tells it.

The control section of the CPU is like the part of your brain that tells you to put one foot in front of the other when you walk. And which way to move your arm when you brush your teeth. And makes your tongue and mouth work together when you talk.

Right, and what the CPU does all the time is *process*—remember that CPU stands for Central *Processing* Unit. So in the CPU, the arithmetic and logic sections *do* the

processing, and the control section tells them *how* to do it and *when* to do it.

Now, the only things we haven't accounted for are: *what* gets processed and *where* is it?

I know the answers to those questions! The CPU processes information *and the information is stored in the computer's* memory.

Good. So now, maybe we ought to go and have a look at *memory.* And since memory is in a different part of the computer, we'll have to take a bus.

25

A bus!

That's right. All the information that gets sent back and forth between the CPU and memory travels along a flat band of wires called a *bus*. There are also buses running from memory to the input and output *ports*.

Ports? Like the ports where ships dock?

Almost. In a computer, a *port* is a place where information from input devices "docks" before catching the bus to memory. And it's where output information leaves the bus to go to one of the output devices. Do you know what these input and output devices are?

*Well, there are terminals . . . and sensors
. . . and disks and tapes.*

Good. So computer memory is like a big bus station, with new information arriving, transferring to other buses, and leaving all the time.

Sounds like a very busy place!

It is. And usually pretty crowded, too. For that reason, most information doesn't stay very long. It's impatient to get where it's going and make room for new information waiting to get in.

What does memory look like?

Well, there are several different kinds of memory. But most of them today use those tiny switches we saw in the CPU. There are thousands of them in memory, and they turn on and off very rapidly as electricity moves through them.

Now, these switches in memory are called *cells*—like brain cells, where all the brain's information is kept.

And these computer memory cells also store information, like the brain. Each cell can hold exactly *one* symbol.

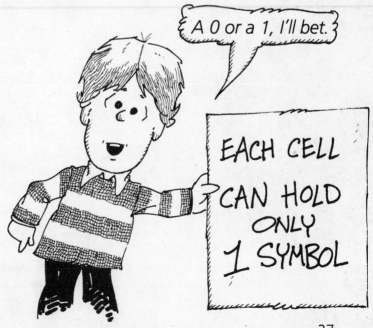

A 0 or a 1, I'll bet.

EACH CELL CAN HOLD ONLY 1 SYMBOL

27

Correct. If the switch is on—which means electricity is passing through it—the cell contains a 1. And if the switch is off—which means there is no electricity going through it—the cell contains a 0.

Does that mean that all the information in the memory cells can be used only for doing arithmetic and making decisions?

No, the binary symbols in memory can also stand for other things, such as letters of the alphabet, and periods, and commas, and dashes and slashes . . . everything that you can find on a typewriter or terminal keyboard.

And *these* symbols can also be put together, to make words, and names and addresses, and even pictures. A computer wouldn't be much good if it could handle only numbers, would it?

Right. You wouldn't be able to read books, or draw pictures, or even talk.

So the cells in computer memory contain binary symbols that stand for many different kinds of information.

But how does the computer know what kind of information all those different 0s and 1s stand for?

It doesn't. It has to be told.

Who tells it?

A *program* does. A program is like the set of directions you get with a kit for building something. Or a recipe you use when you cook. It gives step-by-step instructions on how things are supposed to be done.

But where is the program?

Right there in memory. It's part of a computer's input, from a terminal or a disk. And it's stored in memory until the CPU gets ready to use it. Can you guess which part of the CPU uses the instructions in the program to do its job?

The control section.

Correct. Once the program is stored in memory, the control section of the CPU goes to work. It fetches one instruction at a time from the program, looks to see what the instruction says to do, and chooses the right arithmetic or logic part to do it. Then it goes back to memory to get the next instruction.

If the instruction says to *add* two numbers, it will fetch the numbers from memory and send them to the *arith-*

metic section. If the instruction says to *compare* two numbers, it will send them to the *logic* section. If the command says to *repeat* some of the earlier instructions, it goes back and fetches those instructions from memory all over again.

And all the numbers and things that the program tells the CPU to use—they're all in memory, too, aren't they?

Yes, indeed. They're also part of the computer's input. And they have a name, too—we call them *data*.

So a *program* tells the CPU what *data* to use, and what to do with it. Programs and data are both *input* to the computer, and both are stored in *memory*. Later, we'll see how a program is written, and how it uses the data.

Can there be more than one program in memory at the same time?

Sometimes. In small computers, there's usually only room for one program and some data. But in larger computers, the memory is often divided up into sections, like a parking lot, and each program can take one space.

31

Some computers allow the programs to be divided up into pieces, like a pie. Then the computer will try to fit a few pieces at a time into memory.

Now, to understand how a program can be divided up like this, let's go back to those binary symbols for a minute.

0 and 1, right?

Right. And to computer people, these two symbols are called *bits*. What does the word "bit" make you think of?

Something very small—as in a little bit of something.

Okay, and that's just what it is in a computer—a little bit of information. In fact, it's the smallest piece of information you can have in any program or data. You can't get much smaller than a single 0 or 1!

But bits aren't much use by themselves—they have to be combined to stand for numbers, letters and special characters, periods and commas, for instance. Everything you see on any typewriter or terminal keyboard is made up of a different group of bits.

We even have names for those groups of bits. They're called *bytes*.

Bites?

No, bytes . . . with a "y" instead of an "i." In most computers, there are *eight* bits in a byte. Each letter of the alphabet, for example, takes exactly one byte of space in memory. This means it takes eight bits to make an "A," an "X" or "?."

Sometimes a number is too big to fit into just one byte, so we put several bytes together. And we call this a *word*. A word is usually one or two bytes, but it can be more.

Okay, if you put bits together to make bytes, and you put bytes together to make words, do you get anything if you put words together?

Sure do. Just as you and I put our words together to make sentences, the words in a computer can be put together to make a *record*.

Your school keeps records of all the students—each one's name and address, age, and phone number. Or a record could be one line of a poem. Or one instruction in a program stored in memory.

And I guess you can put records together, too.

Of course—just like your school keeps all the student records together, and the lines of the poem belong together, and the program instructions are stored together in memory. A collection of records is called a *file*.

You mean like in "file cabinet"?

That's right. A file can be any size and is usually made up of records from programs or data. So you can think of computer memory as a sort of file cabinet because it contains the files the CPU is using.

But remember that it's a small file cabinet because computer memory isn't very big. Where do you suppose most of the files are kept?

On the disks and tapes—because they have lots of room.

Correct. And the CPU brings a disk or tape file into its memory only when it needs to use it right away.

Then it puts it back?

It doesn't have to. It only *copies* the file into memory, like you might copy a page from a book onto the blackboard. And the file gets *erased* from memory whenever the CPU brings in a new file—just like erasing the blackboard to make room for the next page of the book.

Now, let's see how much of all this you remember. The smallest piece of information found in computer memory is called a _____.

Bit.

And eight bits together make a _____.

Byte.

And a group of bytes is called a _____.

Word.

And words can be put together to make _____.

Records.

And when we put lots of records together, we get a _____.

Very good. Now you can see how the CPU can separate big files—like some programs—into smaller pieces if the whole thing won't fit into memory. If the whole file has a thousand records, for example, the CPU might use only 200 of them, then replace those by the next 200, and the next, and so on.

Doesn't anything stay in memory all the time?

Some special programs stay there all the time. They have to, just like your brain always remembers certain things—like your name, where you live, how to walk and talk and read. Otherwise, you'd really have a problem!

Do these programs have to be in a special place in memory to keep from getting erased?

Sometimes. But usually they're put in a separate memory altogether.

You mean a computer can have more than one memory?

More than one *kind* of memory—just like your brain. Your brain has a long-term memory that remembers those things we mentioned, like your name and address.

But it also has a short-term memory, which remembers things for only a few minutes or even seconds—like new names and telephone numbers—things you have to write down before you forget.

In a computer, that short-term memory is called *RAM.* RAM is the kind of memory we've been talking about, where most programs keep getting replaced by others

NOW WHAT DID HE SAY HIS NAME WAS?

after they're used. But one special program stays there all the time. That program is called a *monitor,* and it has its own special "parking place" in memory.

We have monitors in school, who help the teachers keep things under control.

That's pretty much what computer monitors do. They make sure all the other programs get sent to the right place in memory, and that they all get a turn to run.

The long-term memory in a computer is called *ROM.* Any program in ROM memory stays there all the time and can't be replaced by another one. On smaller computers, the monitor lives in ROM.

Why doesn't the monitor in bigger computers live in ROM?

Because bigger computers often need more than one monitor. But since only one can be used at a time, you have to be able to put a monitor into memory, and take it out, whenever you want. And you can't do that in ROM.

Why do some computers need more than one monitor? Don't all monitors do the same thing?

In smaller computers, yes. Only one person at a time uses the computer, and the monitor's only job is to input one program at a time into memory.

But the larger, more powerful computers are expected to handle lots of different kinds of jobs. So they need a choice of monitors because each one does something different.

For instance, the computer in a chemical plant controls temperatures in the tanks, and its monitor is called a *real-time* monitor. The computer has to keep checking

the temperatures in the tanks and it has to send back commands right away if any corrections need to be made.

On the other hand, the computer in a hospital probably uses a *time-sharing* monitor. In this kind of system, most of the information is already there, stored on a disk. The monitor allows lots of users with terminals to take turns using that information—except that it all happens so fast that it seems like everyone is using the information at the same time.

Is the monitor a big program?

38

It can be. On large computers, the monitor can take up a big chunk of RAM memory.

On smaller computers, like the ones you find in many homes, the monitor is smaller, too. And it's in ROM, so it doesn't use any of the RAM needed for the program and data.

But now, I think it's time for another quick review. Can you name all the different parts of the computer we've talked about?

Well, there's the CPU. . . .

Which does what?

The arithmetic, and logic . . . and control.

QUIZ
CPU
MEMORY
ROM
RAM
INPUT PORT
OUTPUT PORT

Correct. Next?

The memory . . . and there are two kinds.

Which are?

*ROM, where things don't ever change . . .
and RAM, where programs and data are put
until they're used, and then get erased so
new programs and data can be brought in.*

And what else?

*Input and output ports, where information
comes in from input devices and goes back
out to output devices.*

Good! Another perfect score.

*It's easy to remember when all those parts
are in different places inside the computer,
instead of all mixed together like in the brain.*

Maybe someday those parts of the computer will be
combined. But for the time being, each piece is still on its
own separate *chip.*

What's a chip?

A *chip* is a very thin slice of a special material that can conduct electricity. A chip is about the size of a postage stamp and its electric current can be turned on and off very rapidly.

Like the switches in memory that store binary numbers!

Yes, those switches use the same kind of material. The CPU, memory, and the input and output ports are all on chips because they all process binary information.

In the smallest, simplest computers, everything can actually be on one single, tiny chip. These are used mostly in things like watches and pocket calculators.

But in most computers, there are separate chips for CPU, memory, and input-output ports. They're all connected together on a flat card about the size of an envelope.

On bigger computers, there might be several CPU chips and lots of memory chips on the same card. And on the biggest computers, there may be lots of cards, each with lots of chips. The bigger and more powerful a computer is, the more chips it needs.

Okay, so you've got all these chips to store all the information, and some more chips to do the processing. There's just one thing I still don't understand.

What's that?

How does it all get started? I mean, how do you tell a computer to do all those things? It doesn't speak English, does it?

A few of them do and someday maybe all of them will. But for the time being, we have to do things in a slightly different way. Do you remember what a *program* does?

Yes. You said the CPU uses it to tell the arithmetic section what numbers to add, and the logic section what decisions to make. And it's stored in memory along with the data.

Correct.

*But where does the program come from?
And how does it get into memory? And
what does it look like? And—*

Whoa! One question at a time. Let's start at the top.
We said a program looked sort of like—

*Like a recipe or the directions in a kit for
building something.*

Right, because it's really just a set of instructions. For
example:

RECIPE FOR BOILING EGGS

1. Place eggs in saucepan
2. Add water to cover
3. Bring water to boil
4. Reduce heat to simmer
5. Cook 10-12 minutes
6. Transfer eggs to cold water

DIRECTIONS FOR ASSEMBLING WAGON

1. Fasten axle mount brackets to bottom corners of frame
2. Slide axles through bracket holes
3. Fit wheels onto axle
4. Secure with axle caps
5. Fasten handle bracket to end panel
6. Attach handle to bracket using bolt and nut
7. Peel backing from decals and apply to wagon body

```
PROGRAM TO COMPUTE SALARIES
10   INPUT "HOURS WORKED"; H
20   IF H <=40 THEN LET S = H * 10
     ELSE LET S = (40 * 10) + (H − 40) * 15
30   PRINT "SALARY:   $"; S
40   END
```

Now, what do each of these examples have in common?

Well, each step is very short.

Right. And. . . ?

Each step has a number, to make sure you do them in order.

That's very important. Anything else?

I can't think of anything.

Can any of them be used more than once?

Well, the recipe and directions can. So I guess the program can too.

That's right. And that's probably the most important thing of all. Once it's written down, and *stored* somewhere, the program can be used over and over again, as often as it's needed.

So that's why the program is stored on disk or tape!

Correct. Once it's there, the CPU can copy it into memory as input and use the instructions as many times as it needs.

So we can say that a *program* is a set of instructions that is stored on disk or tape, and is copied into computer memory to tell the CPU what it's supposed to do.

But I still don't know where it came from or how it got there.

Well, just like that recipe, and the directions for assembling the wagon, someone had to write it. And we call that person who writes programs a *programmer.*

That's easy to remember.

Sure it is. The programmer decides just what kind of job the computer is going to have to do, and then writes a set of instructions to tell the computer *step-by-step* how to do it. Just like the person who wrote that recipe had to write down each step to boil the egg.

But you can't write the instructions just any old way. With a computer, you have to say *exactly* what you mean, or it might misunderstand you.

I always say exactly what I mean.

You do, eh? Well, let's see. Suppose you wanted me to find the sum of two numbers—how would you ask me to do it?

Let's see . . . Okay, please add the numbers 8 and 3.

Add them to what?

Well, to each other, of course!

Ah! But you didn't say that, did you? You might have meant for me to add them both to some other number, like 5.

Well, I just thought you would know what I meant.

Actually, I did. But a computer might not. Okay, now what would you do next?

I'd wait for you to give me the answer.

Well, you'd have to wait a long time, because—

I know! Because I didn't tell you to give me the answer.

Right! You only said to add the numbers.
You see? A computer will only do exactly what you tell it—nothing more and nothing less.

Wow! How does the programmer remember all those things?

Lots and lots of practice. But it gets easier after you've done it a few times.
Another very important point is that the instructions must be in exactly the right order. For example, what would happen if we tried to do instruction 3 in the recipe before instruction 2?

What a mess, eh?

Also, all the information must be absolutely correct—even little things.

If someone asked you for directions to the library, for example, what would happen if you told him to turn left instead of right at the traffic light? The person might get hopelessly lost.

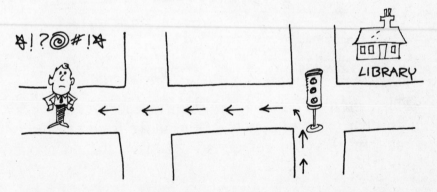

So a computer program must be correct in every way. One little mistake, and the police might arrest an innocent man. Or a rocket might blow up during launch. Or a tank of chemicals could overflow in a factory.

Or a store might charge you too much for something you buy.

That's right. So a programmer usually plans the program very carefully to make sure all the steps are correct and in the right order. This is usually done by drawing a picture of what the program will do.

This picture is called a *flow chart*, because a chart is a kind of map, and to flow means to move from one place to another. Do you remember when we talked about symbols?

Yes. Numbers are made up of symbols, and letters and punctuation marks are symbols because they stand for things.

Well, programmers use symbols in flow charts, too. A rectangle, for example, stands for one step of a program. And inside each rectangle we write what that step does.

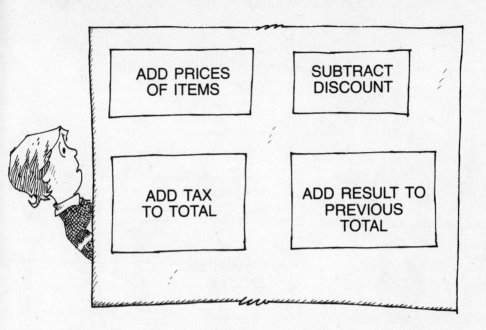

Then we connect the boxes together with arrows to show which ones come first, second, third, and so on.

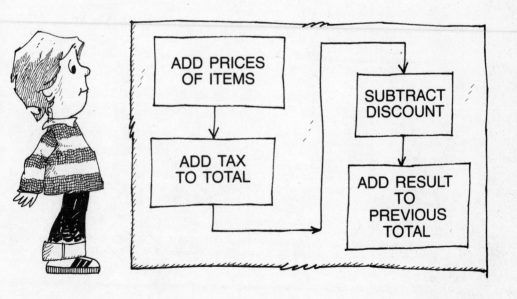

For example, a flow chart for boiling those eggs might look like this:

Notice that some of the short steps have been combined in the flow chart, so we don't end up with too many boxes.

That's because it's a simple recipe. But let's change it a little bit. Suppose we had a very small pan, just big enough for one egg.

Then we'd have to do the recipe more than once.

So we add another instruction to the recipe, saying:

7. Repeat above steps to boil more than one egg

But on the flow chart, we could show this just by adding another arrow:

In computer language, this is called a *loop*.

Because it goes round and round, until you run out of eggs.

Correct. It doesn't matter whether you have a thousand eggs or just one. Once a computer program is placed in memory, the same instructions can be repeated over and over.

> But I see something wrong! The flow chart shows that you keep starting over every time. It doesn't show what happens when you run out of eggs!

Ah, very good point! And if we want our flow chart to be absolutely accurate, we'd better do something about that. What would you suggest?

Add another rectangle?

Not this time. We have a different symbol for cases like this.

Each time we reach the end of the recipe, we'll ask a question: do we have any more eggs? If the answer is YES, an arrow takes us back to the top. If the answer is NO, we quit. So our new symbol looks like this:

This symbol shows that we are making a decision. Does that remind you of anything?

Sure, the logic section of the CPU, where a 1 is a YES and a 0 is a NO.

Good for you. Decision-making is a very important part of a computer's job. And a typical computer program will include lots of decisions.

Let's add another decision to our recipe. Do you know how to recognize a spoiled egg?

Sure, it floats in water.

Right. So let's check to make sure we don't have any bad eggs in the bunch that we're boiling. If there are, they have to be replaced:

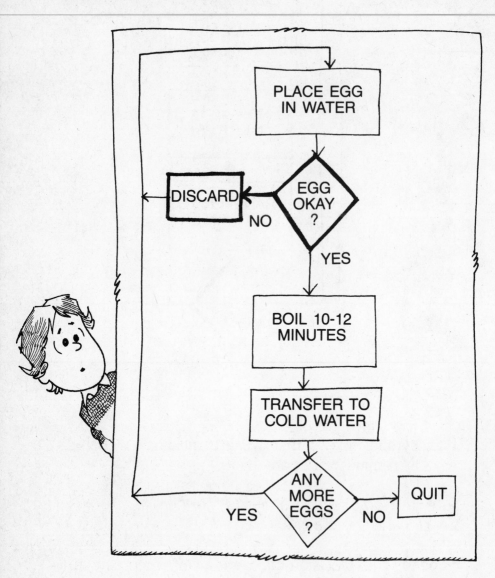

This time, the decision symbol allows us to skip the rest of the program. The NO arrow takes us back to start over with a fresh egg, while the YES arrow allows us to continue as before.

Let's add one more. Suppose we have some big eggs and some small eggs. The big ones take longer to cook than the small ones. How do you think we could test for that?

We'd have to put a decision symbol in before the instruction that tells how long to cook the eggs.

Right. And it would look like this:

So now we've seen that decision symbols in flow charts can tell us when to repeat steps, skip steps and choose between two different steps.

And keep us from repeating the same steps forever!

True, although sometimes that's exactly what we want to do.

It is?

Sure. Think of the computer that measures the temperature of the tanks in the chemical plant. It has to keep measuring even after raising or lowering the temperature:

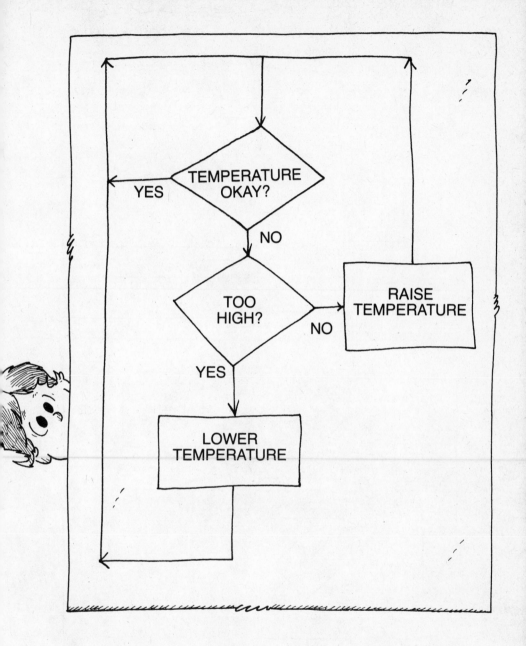

This is called an *endless loop*, because it never stops repeating—unless, of course, the whole system is shut down.

Okay, by now you should be able to draw a flow chart to describe just about any activity you can think of. Why don't you try one?

That's pretty good. But I think you forgot something.

I did? What?

What happens when you keep changing channels and don't find a good program?

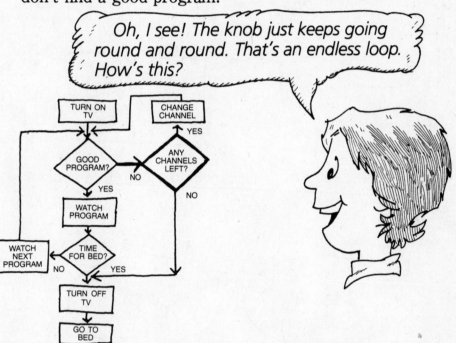

Oh, I see! The knob just keeps going round and round. That's an endless loop. How's this?

That's better. Now you're a flow chart expert.

Are there any other flow chart symbols?

Some programmers use many different ones, such as these:

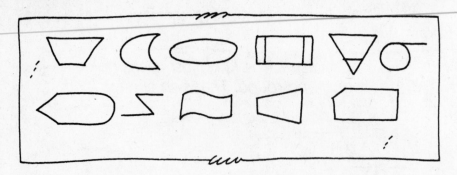

But for most purposes, the fewer the better. We might include

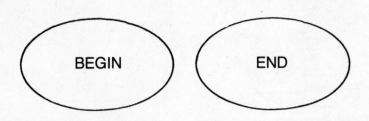

to show where the flow chart starts and stops. And we might need

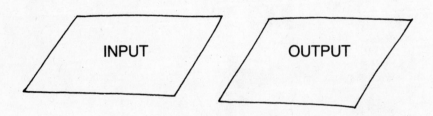

to show where the data comes from and where the answers go.

Suppose I give you two numbers to add. The flow chart might look like this:

Now that's easy, isn't it? But then suppose I gave you a third number—what would you do?

I'd add it to the sum of the first two.

And then if I gave you a fourth?

Same thing. I'd add that number to the new sum.

And if I kept on giving you more numbers?

I'd keep on adding each one to the sum.

Until. . . ?

Until you stopped giving me new numbers.

Correct. Think you could flow chart that?

I can try. How about this:

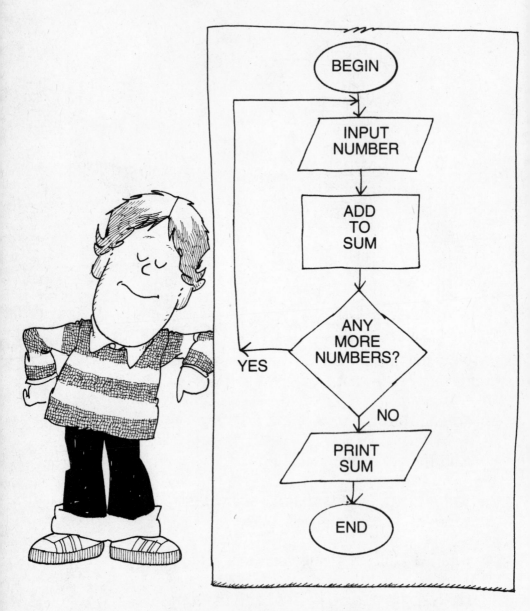

Very good! Now, do you know what an average is? Like the average age of kids in your class?

Sure. We had that problem in school. You add up all the ages and divide by the number of kids. That gives you the average age.

AGE 9   AGE 10   AGE 9   AGE 12

$$9 + 10 + 9 + 12 = 40$$

$$\frac{40}{4} = 10$$

$$10 = \text{AVERAGE AGE}$$

Okay, so let's take those numbers we were adding together and let them stand for the ages of the kids in your class. And after we've found the sum of those ages, we'll divide to find the average.

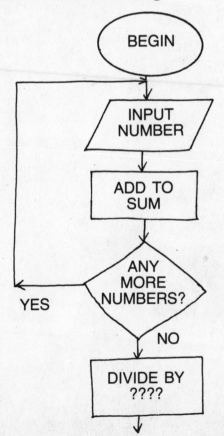

BEGIN

INPUT NUMBER

ADD TO SUM

ANY MORE NUMBERS?

YES

NO

DIVIDE BY ????

Hey—we can't find the average because the flow chart doesn't tell us how many ages we added together! So we don't know what number to divide by.

You're absolutely right. And if we wanted to use the flow chart for a different class, there might be a different number of students.

So what do we do?

Well, suppose you were adding a lot of numbers together and you needed to know how many there were. What would *you* do?

I guess I'd have to keep a count of the numbers while I was adding them.

Well, we should be able to do the same thing in our flow chart. Let's add a "counter" box to our flow chart, and put a 0 in it. Then every time we add a new person's age to our sum, we'll add a 1 to the counter as well.

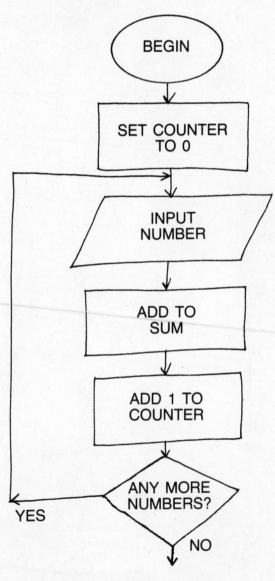

Then after we've added in the last person's age, the counter should tell us how many ages we added together in all.

Then we can divide the sum by the counter to get the average!

Correct. Now, since we need to set the counter to 0 when we start, we need to set the sum to 0 as well. And now our flow chart will look like this:

Now, this is closer to what a real flow chart would look like, if a programmer drew it.

Of course. A carpenter wouldn't build a house without drawing a set of house plans.

And a writer usually makes an outline of a book before starting to write.

And an artist makes a sketch of whatever is going to be painted.

But when does the programmer start writing the program?

As soon as he or she is sure the flow chart is correct. Then the programmer decides which language is best for the program.

Language? You mean like French or German?

No, I mean like FORTRAN or COBOL.

I've never heard of those languages. They only teach French and German and Spanish in our school.

French and German and Spanish are languages that are spoken as well as written. You study them so you can talk to people who speak those languages and read the things they have written.

FORTRAN and COBOL are computer languages and are only written. But they do the same thing—they let you communicate with the computer because the computer doesn't speak English.

Why does the computer need two languages?

Oh, there are lots more than just two! There are over a thousand different computer languages. FORTRAN and COBOL are just a couple of the more popular ones.

The reason that there are so many is because a computer has to do lots of different kinds of jobs. And some languages are better for certain jobs, and others are better for other jobs.

Just like a carpenter uses a tool that works best for a particular job, a programmer uses the language that is best for the problem that needs to be solved.

Think of all the different applications there are for computers. The computer in a chemical plant probably uses a language like FORTRAN because it's designed for scientific kinds of work.

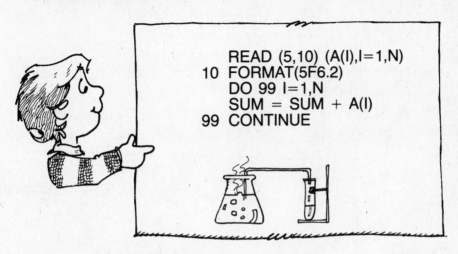

```
      READ (5,10) (A(I),I=1,N)
10    FORMAT(5F6.2)
      DO 99 I=1,N
      SUM = SUM + A(I)
99    CONTINUE
```

And the computer in the bank might use COBOL, which is good for managing bank accounts.

```
READ INPUT-FILE
IF TOTAL-PAY IS LESS THAN MAX
    ADD OVERTIME-PAY TO
    TOTAL-PAY
ADD WEEKPAY TO REGISTER.
CLOSE INPUT-FILE
```

Does each computer have to know all the languages?

The computer doesn't have to know any of them. Do you know what an *interpreter* is?

I think it's a person who listens to someone talk in one language and repeats it to somebody else in another language.

That's right. At the United Nations, for example, when someone from one country makes a speech, there are interpreters to translate it into other languages so everyone can understand what's being said.

Well, a computer has an interpreter, too. It's called a *compiler.*

A compiler is another kind of program that stays in memory. Its job is to read the program in whatever language the programmer used and translate it for the computer.

Translate it into what?

Don't you remember how all the information in the computer is stored?

Oh, yes—in binary.

Right. The programmer can't write the program in binary, so he uses one of the many programming languages we mentioned.

Then the compiler looks at each instruction in the program, translates it into binary, and stores it in computer memory until the CPU gets ready to use it.

Here's what a program might look like, after it's been compiled into binary and stored in memory:

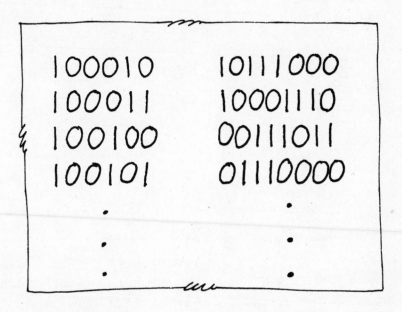

The numbers on the right are the instructions and the ones on the left are their *addresses*.

Addresses? Like addresses on houses?

That's right. Each location in memory that stores a number or a character has an address so that the CPU can find it.

And since program instructions are also stored in memory, they have addresses, too.

Address	Instruction
34	READ NEW NUMBER
35	ADD TO SUM
36	ADD ONE TO COUNT
37	GO TO 22
.	.
.	.
.	.

Also notice that the addresses are in order, just like house numbers along a street. That way, when the compiler tells the CPU the address of the first instruction, the CPU can just add 1 to get the address to get the next instruction . . . and the next one, and the next one, and so on.

Just like the counter in the flow chart!

Exactly. Now, maybe we ought to review some of these ideas, so you won't forget them.

You're a programmer and you have to write a program. What's the first thing you do?

And what's the next step?

Pick the computer language that will do the job the best.

Fine. Once you've written the program, where do you put it?

On disk or tape, until it's ready to run.

And then?

Then the compiler translates it into binary and copies it into computer memory.

And how does the CPU find the program in memory?

The compiler tells it the address.

Very good. We can even flow chart the whole operation:

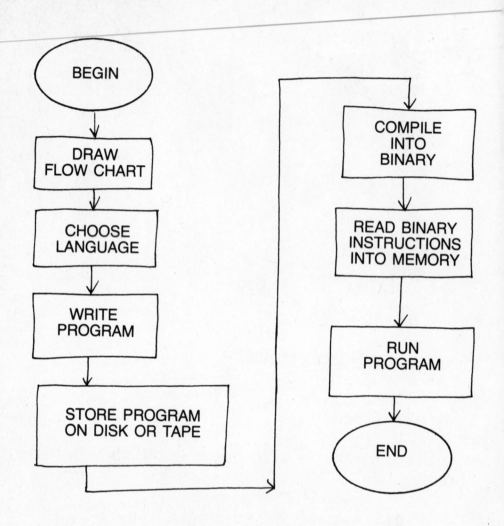

Flow charts look easy, but I'll bet the programs are hard to write.

Some of them are very hard and take lots of time. Professional programmers, who know lots of languages and have lots of experience, tackle these.

But there are some languages that are very easy to learn and they can be used to write simple programs. The most popular one is called BASIC.

It even sounds easy.

It's used on most home computers and is often taught in courses in schools that have computers. And it uses commands that are easy to understand and use.

Here's a very simple BASIC program:

```
10    LET A = 9
20    LET B = 3
30    LET C = 11
40    LET D = A + B + C
50    PRINT D
60    END
```

This program tells the CPU to add the numbers 9, 3 and 11 together, and print out the answer. Do you remember what we call numbers that are processed by the CPU?

I think it was data.

And the part of the CPU that adds the data values together?

The arithmetic section.

Good.

What do the A's and B's and C's mean?

They stand for those addresses in memory we talked about. The data will be stored at these addresses so the CPU can find them.

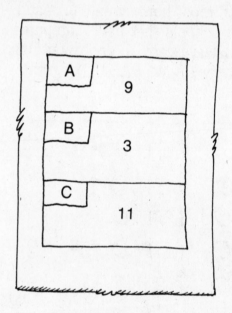

BASIC lets us use letters for addresses, and that's helpful because they're easier to remember. Later, the compiler will change the letter addresses into number addresses.

But now suppose we wanted to add three other numbers—say 2, 14 and 6. Would this program still work?

No, because it says to add 9, 3 and 11. We'd have to change those numbers in the program.

But then the program would only add 2, 14 and 6! How can we make it add any three numbers we want, without changing it in the program each time?

Simple. Instead of putting the data in the instructions, we'll let the instructions read the data.

Read it from where? Oh, I know—from input.

Exactly. So we'll need an instruction to do that:

```
10    INPUT A, B, C
20    LET D = A+B+C
30    PRINT D
40    END
```

The INPUT instruction will make the program wait for someone to type three numbers on the terminal keyboard. Then that input data will be stored at the addresses A, B and C.

Now, can you guess what the D stands for?

That must be the address where the sum is stored.

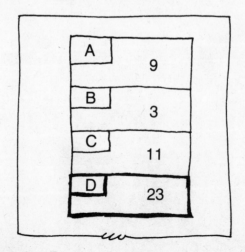

Correct. So the CPU knows where to find the answer when it's ready to print it out.

And I guess that's what the PRINT command does.

Right again. See how simple it is?

Let's do another one. How about the one that finds the average of all the ages?

No sooner said than done:

```
10   INPUT A
20   IF A = 0 GO TO 60
30   LET S = S + A
40   LET K = K + 1
50   GO TO 10
60   V = S / A
70   PRINT S
80   END
```

But there's only one address in the INPUT instruction—and we've got lots of ages to add!

How many spoons do you use to eat a bowl of ice cream? One for each bite?

Of course not! I just use the same one over and over for each bite.

That's what we're doing here—using the same address over and over. Instead of reading all the ages at once, using a different address for each one, we read them one at a time and use the same address each time.

After each person's age is read from the keyboard and

added to the sum, we loop back to the INPUT instruction and read the next one, just like you refill your spoon each time you take a bite.

I guess that saves a lot of space in memory.

Very true. And remember that there isn't much space in memory and we don't want to waste it.

Why does the program ask if A is zero? A person can't be zero years old!

Exactly. We put that number in to tell the CPU that we've reached the end of the list of ages. Otherwise, the computer would just sit there each time, waiting for someone to type the next number.

What do those GO TOs mean?

A GO TO in BASIC is like one of those long arrows in our flow chart:

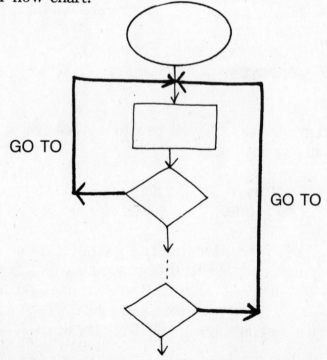

GO TO

GO TO

Remember that the CPU obeys each instruction *in order.* But the first GO TO says IF A is zero, don't go to the next instruction—we're finished, so GO TO the one numbered 60 instead.

```
┌─10 IF A = 0 GO TO 60
│        ·
│        ·
│        ·
└→60 V = S/A
```

And the second GO TO says to go back and repeat instructions 10 through 50, instead of going on to instruction 60.

So that's how we get back to read each new person's age.

Right—that's our loop.

Instruction 30 causes each new age to be added to the sum. And instruction 40 . . . can you guess what it does?

That must be the counter—it adds 1 each time a new person's age is read.

So then we can divide the sum by the counter to find the average, V, and that's what instruction 60 says to do.

And instruction 70 says to print the answer.

Right. So if you've drawn the flow chart carefully, and written all the instructions correctly, the program will always work. The computer will always give you the right answer, no matter how much input you use.

What if I make a mistake when I write the program? What does the computer do then?

Everybody makes mistakes once in a while. And a mistake in a program could cause the wrong information to come out in the end.

If that happens, then the programmer has to find the mistake in the program and correct it. Mistakes in programs are called *bugs*.

Bugs?

That's right. And so the process of tracking down and correcting the bugs is called *debugging*. If the program is a long and complicated one, debugging can be a very difficult task.

Fortunately, there are things in the computer that help the programmer to debug his program. For example, the *compiler* looks carefully at each instruction before translating it into binary. If it contains a word or symbol it doesn't recognize, it prints out a message to the programmer.

If, for example, we had written the word PRIMT in the BASIC program instead of PRINT, the compiler would have told us about it before we went on.

And there are other *system programs* that allow the programmer to examine the binary code in memory after the program has been compiled. Or to do one instruction at a time until the bug is found.

What's a system program?

A system program is one that stays in memory to help your program to run. The monitor is a system program— do you remember what it does?

Yes. It makes sure all the other programs get put in the right place and get a turn to run.

That's right. And some monitors can actually help to debug the program.

But the monitor does a lot more than that. It's sort of like a librarian at a very busy public library. If we think of the computer itself as a library, then all the books are—

Programs!

Right. Now, every time someone writes a new program, it's like when the library gets a new book. And just as the librarian stores the book on the proper shelf, the monitor stores the program—

On disk or tape.

And running a program is like checking out a book. You tell the librarian what book you want, and he fetches it for you—just as the monitor fetches the program from disk or tape.

Then the book has to be taken to the check-out desk . . . just like a program has to be copied into—

Memory.

Right. Then the librarian stamps a date in the book and gives it to you. In the computer, the monitor calls in the compiler, and then turns the binary program over to the CPU.

When I'm finished with the book, I take it back to the library and check out another one.

And the librarian returns it to the stacks and gets a new one for you; in the same way, the monitor replaces the old program in memory with a new one.

And if I have a question?

Whenever you need information, you ask the librarian; in the computer, you ask the monitor.

In all places where computers are used, we see people typing on terminals. They are

> *entering* data into the computer
> *requesting* data from the computer
> *writing* a program
> or *running* a program.

All of these duties are carried out by the monitor.

But who writes the monitor?

Experienced programmers do. The monitor is still a program and computers can't do anything without programs.

WHERE'S MY PROGRAM?

And since people write programs, that means computers can't do anything without people.

Very true. And speaking of writing, you still have that school report to finish. Better hop to it!

GLOSSARY

Address — A numbered location in computer memory where bytes of information are stored.

BASIC — A programming language which is simple to learn and use, found on most computers.

Binary — A counting system, used by computers, in which all numbers are represented by two symbols, 0 and 1.

Bit — A single 0 or 1 in a binary representation of a number or unit of information.

Bug — An error in a computer program; finding and correcting the error is called *debugging*.

Bus — The path by which data is sent between computer memory and the input and output ports.

Byte — A group of bits used to represent a single number, letter or special character in the computer.

Chip — A tiny plate of material that can store information in the form of electrical signals.

Compiler — A system program that translates other programs into binary code so they can be understood by the computer.

Control — The section of the CPU that reads and carries out the instructions of a program.

Counter — A variable, usually set to 0 at the start, to which the CPU adds 1 each time an operation is repeated.

CPU — Central Processing Unit; the part of the computer that performs arithmetic, logic and control operations.

Data — Information used by a program or produced by a program.

Decimal — A counting system in which all numbers are represented by one or more of the following symbols: 0, 1, 2, 3, 4, 5, 6, 7, 8, 9.

File — A collection of records containing similar information, such as names of students in a school or costs of items in a store.

Flow chart — A diagram showing the operations to be performed by a program.

Input — Information that is put into the computer to be processed by a program.

Logic — The section of the CPU that makes decisions which can be answered by a YES or NO.

Loop — A portion of a program that is repeated a specified number of times.

Memory — The area within the computer where information (data and programs) is stored as it is being used by the CPU.

Monitor — A program, often stored in ROM, that supervises the transfer of information in and out of a computer and controls the running of programs by the computer. (Note: the term "monitor" is often used to refer to the terminal screen as well.)

Output — Information transferred out of the computer for display, storage or control.

Port — The part of the computer where input information arrives to be used by the CPU, or output information leaves to be displayed, stored or used for control.

Program — A set of step-by-step instructions that tells the CPU what to do with information provided by a user.

Programmer — A person who writes programs to be run on a computer.

RAM — Random Access Memory; the portion of computer memory where input information (programs and data) may be stored as it is being used.

Record — A collection of words or bytes that represents a piece of useful information, such as a name, address or cost of a single item.

ROM — Read Only Memory; the portion of computer memory containing programs that cannot be changed.

Symbol — A sign or figure that stands for something else; in a computer, 0 and 1 are symbols that can stand for numbers or for NO and YES.

System program — A computer program that aids the user in performing certain processing tasks; the monitor and compiler are examples of system programs.

Terminal — A piece of computer equipment with a typewriter keyboard and a video screen, used for communicating with the computer.

Word — A basic unit of information in the computer, usually one or two bytes in size but occasionally larger.

FIRST LOOK BOOK #3

COMPUTERS:
Menus, Loops and Mice

by J.M. Johnston
Illustrated by Len Epstein

In First Look Book #3, author J.M. Johnston tells how numerous programs are written and used to perform various tasks. With lively illustrations and clear descriptions, *Computers: Menus, Loops and Mice* explains how computers can compose music, generate color pictures and teach math, spelling and composition. It also takes a look at the future, extending computer applications to automated traffic control, home systems, robots and health care.

• •

Please send me _____ copies of **FIRST LOOK BOOK #3**, *Computers: Menus, Loops and Mice*. I am enclosing $3.45 per copy (includes 50¢ postage and handling).
Please send check or money order (no cash or C.O.D.s).

Name _____
(Please Print)
Address _____ Apt. _____
City _____
State _____ Zip _____
Please allow 6-8 weeks for delivery. PA residents add 6% sales tax.

Do you (or your family) own a personal computer?
  ☐ YES   ☐ NO

If so, what kind? _____

Please send this coupon to:
BANBURY BOOKS
37 West Avenue, Suite 201, Wayne, PA 19087